Heroes for Young Readers

Written by Renee Taft Meloche
Illustrated by Bryan Pollard

Adoniram Judson
Amy Carmichael
Betty Greene
Cameron Townsend
Corrie ten Boom
David Livingstone
Eric Liddell
George Müller

Gladys Aylward
Hudson Taylor
Jim Elliot
Jonathan Goforth
Lottie Moon
Mary Slessor
Nate Saint
William Carey

Heroes of History for Young Readers

Written by Renee Taft Meloche
Illustrated by Bryan Pollard

Clara Barton
George Washington
George Washington Carver
Meriwether Lewis

...and more coming soon

*Heroes for Young Readers Activity Guides and audio CDs
are now available! See the back of this book for more information.*

For a free catalog of books and materials contact
YWAM Publishing, P.O. Box 55787, Seattle, WA 98155
1-800-922-2143, www.ywampublishing.com

HEROES FOR YOUNG READERS

BETTY GREENE

Flying High

Written by Renee Taft Meloche
Illustrated by Bryan Pollard

YWAM
PUBLISHING
P.O. BOX 55787   SEATTLE, WA 98155

Betty Greene: Flying High   Text © 2004 by Renee Taft Meloche   Illustrations © 2004 by Bryan Pollard
Published by YWAM Publishing, P.O. Box 55787, Seattle, WA 98155   ISBN 1-57658-239-6   Printed in China.   All rights reserved.

In nineteen forty-one, a tall
　　young woman, Betty Greene,
became a pilot—something that
　　had been her childhood dream.

She'd tried to study nursing—
　　a wonderful career—
but Betty longed instead to fly
　　high through the atmosphere.

She spent long hours learning how
　　to fly a large float plane
that sat upon the surface of
　　a lake where Betty trained.

She loved to see the forceful jets
    of water that would spray
behind her as she pulled back on
    the joystick. Right away
the plane would lift off from the lake;
    before long she could see
her home along Lake Washington.
    The view was heavenly.

She also had another dream:
    she loved God, and she prayed
that He would use her to do Christian
    mission work someday.

America was forced one day
     to enter World War II.
The military needed help
     from women pilots who
could fly planes with great competence
     in fairly safe conditions,
and who would not be put in danger
     flying combat missions.

So Betty joined these women and
     she found it challenging.
For passing all the flying drills,
     she soon earned silver wings!

Among her jobs, she pulled a target
     right behind her plane,
so soldiers on the ground could practice
     shooting with sharp aim.

Her first time up, live shells began
     exploding all around.
A soldier—quite mistakenly—
     was trying to shoot her down!

But fortunately someone radioed
     the urgent news:
"We're being shelled! Please stop the one
     who's utterly confused!"

She also was assigned to test
        equipment that was new
and check a plane's performance out
        while at high altitude.

Though Betty knew how dangerous
        it was to do these tests,
her flying skills had proved to be
        among her unit's best.

The war was not quite over when,
        in nineteen forty-four,
her unit was disbanded, not
        being needed anymore.

But Betty knew instinctively
        what her next step would be
when asked to start a brand-new group—
        a flying ministry.

The pilots would help missionaries
        get from place to place
and help them with emergencies
        they frequently would face.

This seemed a gift from heaven, then,
        for Betty Greene to find
her love of God and love of flying
        perfectly combined.

She flew the group's red biplane down
        to southern Mexico
from California, just the first
        of many spots she'd go.

She flew into a jungle camp
    and brought the missionaries
supplies and precious mail from home,
    then offered to help ferry
them over hills and jungle to
    get visas for Peru—
a country they would enter soon
    for new work they would do.

Five years passed by; then in the year
        of nineteen fifty-one,
she flew into Nigeria
        beneath a blazing sun.

While there, a missionary with
        her newborn son in tow
asked Betty if she'd fly them home.
        She gladly said she'd go
and took off upward toward blue sky.
        The day was clear and bright.
The plane was purring like a cat.
        Below them was the sight
of the Sahara Desert with
        its vast expanse of sand.
They spotted several camels; all
        was going just as planned.

As Betty looked into the distance,
though, something appeared
that looked like one big cloud of dust,
but as the cloud grew near
it looked more like a wall of sand.
Soon she could barely see.
She tried to stay calm even though
her heart beat rapidly.

She realized now the wind was whipping
    sand up off the ground
and pelting it against her windshield.
    She flew lower down
and skimmed along the surface, trying
    to find a place to land.
But all around were miles of dunes
    and piles of desert sand.

Then from within the golden swirl
        of sand, as Betty prayed,
her eyes made out a welcome sight:
        a road made of red clay.

The road became her lifeline and
        her straight and narrow guide.
She followed it until the road
        grew wider and she spied
a small airport—a miracle!
        She landed late that day:
though she was blinded in the storm
        her God had shown the way.

When after two more days the sandstorm
        finally had passed,
she flew the missionary and
        her baby home at last.

Then later Betty headed to
    an island, unexplored—
New Guinea—where some missionaries
    told about the Lord.

The people of New Guinea lived
    in villages well hidden,
surrounded by the mountains and
    lush trees that God had given.

Inside the jungle, people built
    an airstrip for small planes,
so missionaries would not have
    to trek over terrain
of rugged mountain forests that
    took days to struggle through.
But first the airstrip had to be
    inspected—it was new.

So Betty, with one other woman
        and some native guides,
decided she would walk across
        the dangerous mountainside,
despite the risk of injury
        and knowing she could face
an ambush by the tribesmen who
        inhabited the place.

They set out, and as Betty climbed
        a steep hill—nice and slow—
she saw a river flowing through
        thick jungle down below.

A footbridge lay ahead of her—
        made only of thin vines.
She'd have to walk across that way
        or she'd be left behind.

She slid her hands along the rails
        of vines, but broke a sweat
when some of them began to snap!
        With fear, she took small steps.

She finally crossed the flimsy bridge
        and then continued on.
She clambered up some mountain ridges
        that were steep and long.

Then at the top of one ridge, she
　　looked down the other side:
a village was in flames—there was
　　a war among the tribes.

She saw some tribesmen with long spears
　　and hid behind a tree.
But Betty's guides proceeded down—
　　with great care, cautiously—
and soon returned with news that all
　　the warriors gave permission
for them to pass unharmed and to
　　continue on their mission.

As Betty and her team pressed on,
    they hiked for several days.
They climbed up one last ridge and then,
    beneath the final rays
of sun, they saw the airstrip and
    a mission post below.
They hastened down the ridge; at last
    it wasn't far to go.

When Betty checked the airstrip out,
    she searched it up and down
for obstacles, soft spots, and holes—
    or pitfalls in the ground.

The strip passed her inspection—
    it was in quite good shape—
which meant that missionaries would
    no longer have to make
the tortuous trip through jungle mountains
    they had often tread.
They now could travel fast—in comfort—
    in a plane instead.

Then after news was sent out that
　　the airstrip was okay,
a humming sound grew louder in
　　the forest that same day.

And soon the noise was overhead.
　　The native people cheered
and danced and celebrated as
　　a Cessna plane appeared.

And as it landed on the airstrip,
　　Betty felt glad too,
along with all the missionaries
　　for—relieved—they knew
the plane would be a lifeline when
　　they needed medical care
or food or news or even urgent
　　exit out of there.

Now Betty kept on making flights
    to jungle mission stations,
until she went back home and spoke
    to many congregations
about her great adventures flying
    high up in the skies,
and even more importantly
    helped them to realize
just what a single airplane to
    a missionary meant.
By bringing gifts of care and help,
    a plane seemed heavensent.

At seventy-six in nineteen
    ninety-seven, Betty died.
But her good work lives on as airplanes
    now are used worldwide
to give the missionaries wings,
    to help their spirits soar,
as other pilots now continue
    flights as flown before.

If we can use our gifts for God
    as Betty did, in flight,
then like her plane, we too can be
    a helpful, welcome sight.

Christian Heroes: Then & Now

by Janet and Geoff Benge

Adoniram Judson: Bound for Burma
Amy Carmichael: Rescuer of Precious Gems
Betty Greene: Wings to Serve
Brother Andrew: God's Secret Agent
Cameron Townsend: Good News in Every Language
Clarence Jones: Mr. Radio
Corrie ten Boom: Keeper of the Angels' Den
Count Zinzendorf: Firstfruit
C. S. Lewis: Man, Myth, and Imagination
C. T. Studd: No Retreat
David Livingstone: Africa's Trailblazer
Eric Liddell: Something Greater Than Gold
Florence Young: Mission Accomplished
George Müller: The Guardian of Bristol's Orphans
Gladys Aylward: The Adventure of a Lifetime
Hudson Taylor: Deep in the Heart of China
Ida Scudder: Healing Bodies, Touching Hearts
Jim Elliot: One Great Purpose
John Wesley: The World as His Parish
John Williams: Messenger of Peace
Jonathan Goforth: An Open Door in China
Lillian Trasher: The Greatest Wonder in Egypt
Loren Cunningham: Into All the World
Lottie Moon: Giving Her All for China
Mary Slessor: Forward into Calabar
Nate Saint: On a Wing and a Prayer
Rachel Saint: A Star in the Jungle
Rowland Bingham: Into Africa's Interior
Sundar Singh: Footprints Over the Mountains
Wilfred Grenfell: Fisher of Men
William Booth: Soup, Soap, and Salvation
William Carey: Obliged to Go

*Heroes for Young Readers and Heroes of History for Young Readers are based on the
Christian Heroes: Then & Now and Heroes of History biographies by Janet and Geoff Benge.
Don't miss out on these exciting, true adventures for ages ten and up!*

Continued on the next page...

Heroes of History
by Janet and Geoff Benge

Abraham Lincoln: A New Birth of Freedom
Benjamin Franklin: Live Wire
Christopher Columbus: Across the Ocean Sea
Clara Barton: Courage under Fire
Daniel Boone: Frontiersman
Douglas MacArthur: What Greater Honor
George Washington Carver: From Slave to Scientist
George Washington: True Patriot
Harriet Tubman: Freedombound
John Adams: Independence Forever
John Smith: A Foothold in the New World
Laura Ingalls Wilder: A Storybook Life
Meriwether Lewis: Off the Edge of the Map
Orville Wright: The Flyer
Theodore Roosevelt: An American Original
Thomas Edison: The Inventor
William Penn: Liberty and Justice for All

...and more coming soon. Unit study curriculum guides are also available.

Heroes for Young Readers Activity Guides
Educational and Character-Building Lessons for Children
by Renee Taft Meloche

Heroes for Young Readers Activity Guide for Books 1–4
Gladys Aylward, Eric Liddell, Nate Saint, George Müller

Heroes for Young Readers Activity Guide for Books 5–8
Amy Carmichael, Corrie ten Boom, Mary Slessor, William Carey

Heroes for Young Readers Activity Guide for Books 9–12
Betty Greene, David Livingstone, Adoniram Judson, Hudson Taylor

Heroes for Young Readers Activity Guide for Books 13–16
Jim Elliot, Cameron Townsend, Jonathan Goforth, Lottie Moon

...and more coming soon.

Designed to accompany the vibrant Heroes for Young Readers books, these fun-filled activity guides lead young children through a variety of character-building and educational activities. Pick and choose from the activities or follow the included thirteen-week syllabus. An audio CD with book readings, songs, and fun activity tracks is available for each Activity Guide.

For a free catalog of books and materials contact
YWAM Publishing, P.O. Box 55787, Seattle, WA 98155
1-800-922-2143, www.ywampublishing.com